# PRENTICE HALL
# WRITING AND GRAMMAR

## Vocabulary and Spelling Practice Book

**Grade Twelve**

Boston, Massachusetts,
Upper Saddle River, New Jersey

Copyright © by Pearson Education, Inc., publishing as Pearson Prentice Hall, Boston, Massachusetts, 02116. All rights reserved. Printed in the United States of America. This publication is protected by copyright, and permission should be obtained from the publisher prior to any prohibited reproduction, storage in a retrieval system, or transmission in any form or by any means, electronic, mechanical, photocopying, recording, or likewise. For information regarding permission(s), write to: Rights and Permissions Department, One Lake Street, Upper Saddle River, New Jersey 07458.

**Pearson Prentice Hall™** is a trademark of Pearson Education, Inc.
**Pearson®** is a registered trademark of Pearson plc.
**Prentice Hall®** is a registered trademark of Pearson Education, Inc.

ISBN 0-13-361609-6

1 2 3 4 5 6 7 8 9 10    10 09 08 07 06

# Contents

**Part 1: Vocabulary Development**

Vocabulary Practice 1: Prefixes *sub-, suc-, suf-, sug-, sus-* .................................................. 1
Vocabulary Practice 2: Prefixes *ig-, il-, im-, in-, ir-* .......................................................... 2
Vocabulary Practice 3: Prefixes *ad-, af-, ag-, al-, an-, ap-, ar-, as-, at-* .................................. 3
Vocabulary Practice 4: Prefixes *macro-, micro-, mega-* ...................................................... 4
Vocabulary Practice 5: Suffixes *-ative, -ive* .................................................................... 5
Vocabulary Practice 6: Suffixes *-ious, -ous* .................................................................... 6
Vocabulary Practice 7: Suffixes *-ate, -id, -ile* .................................................................. 7
Vocabulary Practice 8: Suffixes *-ate, -en, -fy, -ify, -ize* ...................................................... 8
Vocabulary Practice 9: Word Roots *-cred-, -cern-, -cert-* .................................................... 9
Vocabulary Practice 10: Word Roots *-ceive-, -cept-, -cip-* .................................................. 10
Vocabulary Practice 11: Word Roots *-cad-, -cas-, -cid-* ...................................................... 11
Vocabulary Practice 12: Word Roots *-aug- or -aux-, -cre-, -cres-, -cret-* .................................. 12
Vocabulary Practice 13: Word Roots *Latin and Greek Roots* ................................................ 13–14
Vocabulary Practice 14: Synonyms ................................................................................ 15
Vocabulary Practice 15: Synonyms ................................................................................ 16
Vocabulary Practice 16: Synonyms ................................................................................ 17
Vocabulary Practice 17: Antonyms ................................................................................ 18
Vocabulary Practice 18: Antonyms ................................................................................ 19
Vocabulary Practice 19: Antonyms ................................................................................ 20
Vocabulary Practice 20: Synonym and Antonyms ............................................................... 21
Vocabulary Practice 21: Analogies ................................................................................. 22
Vocabulary Practice 22: Analogies ................................................................................. 23
Vocabulary Practice 23: Analogies ................................................................................. 24
Vocabulary Practice 24: Connotations and Denotations ....................................................... 25
Vocabulary Practice 25: Connotations and Denotations ....................................................... 26
Vocabulary Practice 26: Connotations and Denotations ....................................................... 27
Vocabulary Practice 27: Commonly Misused Words ........................................................... 28
Vocabulary Practice 28: Commonly Misused Words ........................................................... 29
Vocabulary Practice 29: Commonly Misused Words ........................................................... 30
Vocabulary Practice 30: Specialized Vocabulary ................................................................. 31
Vocabulary Practice 31: Specialized Vocabulary ................................................................. 32

**Part 2: Spelling Applications**

**Using Spelling Rules**
Spelling Practice 1: Prefixes and Hyphens ........................................................................ 33
Spelling Practice 2: Adding Prefixes ............................................................................... 34–35
Spelling Practice 3: Adding Suffixes ............................................................................... 36–37
Spelling Practice 4: Adding Suffixes ............................................................................... 38

**Practicing Commonly Misspelled Words**
Spelling Practice 5: Doubled Middle Consonants ............................................................... 39–40
Spelling Practice 6: Unpronounced Consonants ................................................................. 41
Spelling Practice 7: Spelling Word Endings ...................................................................... 42
Spelling Practice 8: Spelling Word Endings ...................................................................... 43
Spelling Practice Review ............................................................................................. 44

© Prentice-Hall, Inc.

Name _____  Date _____

# Vocabulary Practice 1: Prefixes

**Prefixes:** *sub-, suc-, suf-, sug-, sus-*

A **prefix** is a word part that is added to the beginning of a base word. A prefix changes the meaning of a word.

The Latin prefix *sub-* means "under," "below," or "secretly." Adding *sub-* to the base word *script*, meaning "letter," makes *subscript*, which means "letter or symbol written below or underneath." Prefixes with the same meaning as *sub-* are *suc-, suf-, sug-,* and *sus-*. These prefixes are parts of words whose spellings have changed over time.

**A.** Add the prefix *sub-* to the word and write the prefixed word with its definition.

| title | culture | species | division | component |
|---|---|---|---|---|
| standard | continent | stratum | committee | temperate |

1. _____ a part resulting from breaking into smaller parts
2. _____ a social group that exhibits behavior that is different from others
3. _____ a part that lies beneath another part and supports it
4. _____ a division of a large landmass
5. _____ a part within a part, especially in equipment
6. _____ a group organized under a larger group for a specific purpose
7. _____ a subordinate or secondary name
8. _____ a biological classification that ranks below a particular kind
9. _____ occurring in the colder areas of the earth's zones
10. _____ falling under the norm

**B.** Use the prefix, word origin, and sentence to write a definition for the boldface word. Check your definitions in a dictionary.

1. *sustain* is *sus-* and *tain* (from *tenere* meaning "to hold")
   The relief organization provided rations to **sustain** the refugees for several weeks.
   _____

2. *suffocate* is *suf-* and *focate* (from *fauces* meaning "throat")
   When the air conditioning in the gym failed, the players and fans thought they would **suffocate.**
   _____

3. *succumb* is *suc-* and *cumb* (from *cumbere* meaning "to lie down")
   Although the doctors worked diligently, the patient **succumbed** to his injuries.
   _____

4. *suggest* is *sug-* and *gest* (from *gerere* meaning "to carry")
   The teacher asked students to **suggest** criteria to evaluate the selection for study.
   _____

5. *susceptible* is *sus-* and *ceptible* (from *capere* meaning "to take")
   With low resistance, the young man was **susceptible** to many illnesses.
   _____

© Prentice-Hall, Inc.

Name _____    Date _____

# Vocabulary Practice 2: Prefixes

**Prefixes:** *ig-, il-, im-, in-, ir-*

   A **prefix** is a word part that is added to the beginning of a base word. A prefix changes the meaning of the word.
   The prefixes *ig-, il-, im-, in-,* and *ir-* mean "not," "into," "on," or "in." Adding *in-* to the base word *accessible*, meaning "attainable," makes *inaccessible*, which means "not attainable."

**A.** Add the base word that belongs with each prefix to make the new word that matches the definition. Check your definitions in a dictionary.

| conceivable | noble   | corrigible | reverent      | pose      |
| pregnable   | logical | luminate   | consequential | revocable |

1. in _____ means "not capable of being corrected"
2. il _____ means "not showing good sense"
3. ir _____ means "not showing the proper respect or seriousness"
4. im _____ "to force on another"
5. ig _____ means "not possessing dignified or outstanding qualities"
6. il _____ means "to give light to"
7. in _____ means "not possible; unthinkable"
8. im _____ "not able to be captured or entered"
9. ir _____ means "not capable of being recalled or altered"
10. in _____ means "not important; irrelevant"

**B.** Add *il-, im-, in-,* or *ir-* to these words and write the new words. Then, write brief definitions for the prefixed words.

responsible _____

practical _____

literate _____

coherent _____

capacity _____

**C.** Write the words from Exercise B in these sentences.

1. Jonah dedicated his life to helping the _____ learn to read and write.
2. The onlookers' ideas for rescue were _____ given the accident conditions.
3. The runners demonstrated an _____ to complete marathons in excessive heat.
4. The coast guard was unable to respond to the _____ message from the distant ship.
5. Seeing the merchandise in disarray, the manager said the employee was _____.

Name _____  Date _____

# Vocabulary Practice 3: Prefixes

**Prefixes:** *ac-, ad-, af-, ag-, al-, an-, ap-, ar-, as-, at-*

   A **prefix** is a word part that is added to the beginning of a base word. A prefix changes the meaning of the word.
   The Latin prefixes *a-, ac-, ad-, af-, ag-, al-, an-, ap-, ar-, as-,* and *at-* mean "to" or "toward." The prefixes *-a* and *-an* also mean "not" and "without." These prefixes are parts of Latin words whose spellings have changed over time. The prefix *ad-* added to the Latin word *mittere*, which means "to send," is now the word *admittance*.

**A.** Underline the prefixes in these words. Then, write the word that completes each sentence. Some words require suffixes.

| alleviate | aggressive | arraign | accost | aggregate |
| adjacent | atrophy | affiliate | assimilate | align |
| appease | ancillary | apathetic | anomalous | adjunct |

1. Scientists _____ with an environmental group met to discuss preservation of water resources.

2. Mary Brown is a psychologist and an _____ professor at the university.

3. A stranger _____ the young man, demanding directions and acting suspiciously.

4. The suspect was _____ on charges of violating motor vehicle statutes.

5. Ed's doctor was concerned that his leg muscles would _____ if he did not exercise.

6. The residents' diverse backgrounds were _____ into a single neighborhood.

7. The mediator was unable to _____ the angry protesters.

8. After completing the principal research, there were many _____ documents that had to be studied.

9. The astronomer explained how the moon and sun _____ for an eclipse.

10. The _____ sales of all the companies exceeded the economists' projections.

**B.** Write the definitions of the words in Exercise A. Then, write a sentence using each word.

_____
_____
_____
_____
_____
_____
_____
_____

© Prentice-Hall, Inc.

Name _____  Date _____

# Vocabulary Practice 4: Prefixes

**Prefixes:** *macro-, micro-, mega-*

    A **prefix** is a word part that is added to the beginning of a base word. A prefix changes the meaning of the word.
    The prefix *macro-* means "large" or "long." Adding *macro-* to *molecule* makes *macromolecule*, which means "a very large molecule." Other prefixes also describe size: *micro-* means "small"; *mega-* means "large" or "great."

**A.** Write a definition for each boldface word. Check your definitions in a dictionary.

1. **microbiology** (*biology* means "relating to living organisms")
   Definition _____

2. **macrofossil** (*fossil* means "a remnant of a past living organism")
   Definition _____

3. **microeconomics** (*economics* means "related to money, finances")
   Definition _____

4. **megadose** (*dose* means "a measured quantity")
   Definition _____

5. **microscope** (*scope* means "an instrument for viewing")
   Definition _____

6. **macroscale** (*scale* means "a tool to measure weight")
   Definition _____

7. **microsurgery** (*surgery* means "work done by a doctor or surgeon")
   Definition _____

8. **megafauna** (*fauna* means "animal life")
   Definition _____

9. **microorganism** (*organism* means "a living being")
   Definition _____

10. **megavitamin** (*vitamin* means "an organic substance containing nutrients")
    Definition _____

**B.** Add the prefix *macro-*, *micro-*, or *mega-* to each word. Then, write the definitions for the words. Check your definitions in a dictionary.

1. _____ film _____
2. _____ watt _____
3. _____ ton _____
4. _____ evolution _____
5. _____ biotic _____
6. _____ processor _____

4  Vocabulary Practice 4: Prefixes          © Prentice-Hall, Inc.

Name _____  Date _____

# Vocabulary Practice 5: Suffixes

**Suffixes:** *-ative, -ive*

A **suffix** is a word part added to the end of a word that changes the word's meaning.

The suffixes *-ive* and *-ative* mean "of, relating to, or tending to." Adding *-ive* to the word *contemplate*, meaning "to think about intently," makes *contemplative*, which means "of, or inclined to thoughtful inspection."

**A.** Underline the word in each sentence with the suffix *-ive* or *-ative*. Then, choose the definition for each word and write the letter of the definition at the end of the sentence.

a. tending to fight
b. tending to escape understanding
c. tending to remove from serious consideration
d. relating to being sharp or pointed
e. tending to stimulate

f. tending to be curious
g. relating to the positive
h. relating to words having repeated initial sounds
i. relating to take advantage
j. tending to protect against spoilage

1. The inquisitive young woman enjoyed challenging her teachers with questions. _____
2. Ms. Brown's affirmative approach to discipline made her popular with students. _____
3. Readers were frustrated and confused by the book's elusive plot. _____
4. The alliterative title, *Masked Marauder in the Mist,* piqued Mark's curiosity. _____
5. A combative teenager leaped from his car to yell at another driver. _____
6. Exploitive businesses have collected large sums of money from trusting clients. _____
7. The chef acknowledged the need for preservative agents in some perishable foods. _____
8. With a dismissive shake of the head, the teacher rejected the student's answer. _____
9. One nurse's incisive letter got to the heart of the hospital's problems. _____
10. The provocative speech prompted many in the audience to sign the petition. _____

**B.** On another piece of paper, write five more words with the suffixes *-ive* and *-ative* and their definitions.

© Prentice-Hall, Inc.

Name _____  Date _____

# Vocabulary Practice 6: Suffixes

**Suffixes:** *-ious, -ous*

A **suffix** is a word part added to the end of a base word that changes the meaning of the word. The suffixes *-ious* and *-ous* mean "full of," "having," "possessing the qualities of," or "characterized by." Adding *-ous* to the base word *poison*, meaning "a substance that kills or injures through its chemical action," makes *poisonous*, which means "possessing the ability to kill or injure through chemical action."

**A.** Add the suffix *-ious* or *-ous* to each word and write the new word. Some words change spelling before adding the suffix. Check your spelling in a dictionary.

1. acrimony _____
2. malice _____
3. circuit _____
4. pore _____
5. moment _____
6. fallacy _____
7. clamor _____
8. audacity _____
9. cacophony _____
10. content _____

**B.** Use the suffixed words in Exercise A to complete these sentences.

1. Several _____ neighbors argued about everything from barking dogs to trash disposal.
2. June's _____ letter to the editor shocked many newspaper readers.
3. The girl did not understand the line between practical jokes and _____ pranks.
4. Rather than taking the scenic, _____ route, our taxi driver took the highway.
5. The _____ shrieking birds at the pet store annoyed the customers next door.
6. The witness made a _____ statement, implicating an innocent person.
7. Eric's plans seemed so _____ that no one believed he would succeed.
8. The carpenter chose a _____ wood that would absorb the stain quickly.
9. Jim's high school graduation was a _____ occasion for his entire family.
10. The _____ fans demanded an encore and would not quit their noise.

**C.** Add the suffix *-ious* or *-ous* to the word to form a new word. Write a brief definition of the suffixed word.

| **Word** | **Word with Suffix** |
|---|---|
| 1. avarice | avaric _____ |
| 2. predator | predac _____ |
| 3. volume | volumin _____ |
| 4. pendant | pendul _____ |
| 5. judgment | judic _____ |

Name _____ Date _____

# Vocabulary Practice 7: Suffixes

**Suffixes:** *-ate-, -id, -ile*

A **suffix** is a word part added to the end of a base word that changes the meaning of the word. The Latin suffixes *-ate*, *-id*, and *-ile* mean "state or quality of" and form adjectives. Adding *-ate* to the word *consider* makes *considerate*, which means "the state of treating in an attentive way." Adding the suffix *-ile* to the word *infant* makes *infantile*, which means "suitable for or characteristic of infants." The suffix *-id* appears at the end of many derived words, such as *intrepid*, from the Latin word *intrepidus*.

**A.** Add *-ate*, *-id*, or *-ile* to complete the boldface word. Then, write the suffixed word and its definition. Check your words in a dictionary.

1. Roz was an **av**_____ reader with a rich and interesting speaking vocabulary.
   Definition_____

2. Although unable to speak the language, Althea was **liter**_____ in Spanish.
   Definition_____

3. The judge decided that the neighborhood residents had a **legitim**_____ complaint.
   Definition_____

4. The athlete's **passion**_____ speech moved the crowd to a thunderous applause.
   Definition_____

5. Denyce's **serv**_____ attitude did not impress her supervisor.
   Definition_____

6. The young boy's imagination gave life to **inanim**_____ objects.
   Definition_____

7. Adopted from the pound, Shelby was not **doc**_____ at first, but adjusted quickly.
   Definition_____

8. Ken was an **intrep**_____ traveler, venturing to areas infrequented by tourists.
   Definition_____

9. Exercise and a good diet help elderly people remain **ag**_____ and healthy.
   Definition_____

10. A **volat**_____ situation was thwarted through arbitration.
    Definition_____

**B.** Write a sentence using each phrase or your own.

1. **rabid** dog _____

2. **valid** argument _____

3. **tactile** example _____

4. **placid** lake _____

5. **consummate** player _____

© Prentice-Hall, Inc.

Name _____  Date _____

# Vocabulary Practice 8: Suffixes

**Suffixes:** *-ate, -en, -fy, -ify, -ize*

   A **suffix** is a word part added to the end of a base word. A suffix changes the meaning of the word.
   The verb suffix *-en* means "to cause to be or cause to have" or "to come to be or come to have." Adding *-en* to *fright*, meaning "fear," makes *frighten*, which means "to cause to have fear." The suffixes *-ate, -fy, -ify,* and *-ize* also change words to verbs. The suffix *-ate* is also used to change words to adjectives. The suffix *-ate* means "to cause to become;" "to furnish with"; *-fy, -ify* mean "to make," "to form into," "to invest with the attributes of"; *-ize* means "to cause to be or to conform to" or "to resemble."

**A.** Add the suffix *-ate, -en, -fy, -ify,* or *-ize* to the boldface word or word part to make the word that matches the definition. Use the dictionary to check your words.

1. **amelior** _____ to cause to become better
2. **rect** _____ to make right
3. **ostra** _____ to banish or exclude by consensus
4. **height** _____ to cause to be larger, or in a higher position
5. **obliter** _____ to cause to become imperceptible
6. **moll** _____ to soothe or pacify
7. **steep** _____ to cause to be steep, or precipitous
8. **synchron** _____ to cause to happen, exist, or arise at precisely the same time
9. **null** _____ to cause or make worth nothing
10. **desensit** _____ to make less reactive to

**B.** Write the boldface words in Exercise A in these sentences. Some words require a tense change.

1. In ancient Greece, individuals were _____ by a general vote of the population.
2. The teacher tried to _____ the learning environment by inviting guest speakers.
3. The dancers _____ their movements to leap into the air on the last note.
4. Tim's interest in the article _____ when he read a name he recognized.
5. The noisy airport nearby _____ the children to the sounds of traffic.
6. The path _____ near the old quarry—the site of several hiking accidents.
7. The cashier _____ the angry crowd by issuing rain checks for the sold-out items.
8. The urgent call was _____ by a downed telephone wire.
9. He tried to _____ the error by paying the disputed amount.
10. A tornado _____ an entire section of the town.

Name _____    Date _____

# Vocabulary Practice 9: Word Roots

**Word Roots:** *-cred-, -cern-, -cert-*

A **word root** forms the basic part of all words and gives the word its primary meaning. Knowing the meaning of a word root can help you determine the meaning of the whole word.

The word root *-cert-* means "sure." The adjective *certain* means "to be sure." Other word roots similar in meaning to *-cert-* are *-cred-*, which means "trust" or "believe," and *-cern-*, which means "perceive," "decide," or "make certain."

**A.** Write the word that completes each sentence. Underline the word root in each answer choice.

1. New members of the club read the _____ for being a good citizen.

    **concern**      **creed**      **credence**

2. Grandfather told me with _____ that he would be skiing on his 100th birthday.

    **credibility**      **credit**      **certainty**

3. Because of power failure, we were unable to _____ the exact time the tornado hit.

    **ascertain**      **uncertain**      **certitude**

4. Students were advised not to give _____ to the rumors about the school fire.

    **certitude**      **credence**      **discernment**

5. Several _____ doctors volunteered their time to the relief effort.

    **discredit**      **uncertain**      **concerned**

6. Despite a dearth of evidence, the jury found the prosecutor's arguments _____.

    **credence**      **credible**      **discernible**

7. Competitive sports officials can _____ the winning time to a split second.

    **credit**      **discredit**      **certify**

8. When Jason was told that he had won the lottery, he was _____!

    **incredulous**      **indiscernible**      **incredible**

9. Stewart's _____ makes him a great leader in a survival course.

    **credible**      **uncertainty**      **discernment**

10. Hank's citizenship is _____ because he has his naturalization papers.

    **certifiable**      **disconcerting**      **credited**

**B.** On another piece of paper, explain why each choice in 1–10 is correct, referring to the meaning of the root in your answer.

© Prentice-Hall, Inc.

Name _____  Date _____

# Vocabulary Practice 10: Word Roots

**Word Roots:** *-ceive-, -cept-, -cip-*

    A **word root** forms the basic part of all words and gives the word its primary meaning. Knowing the meaning of a word root can help you determine the meaning of the whole word.
    The root *-ceive-* means "take" or "receive," as in the word *perceive*, which means "to take awareness or understanding." The roots *-cept-* and *-cip-* also mean "take" or "receive."

**A.** Circle the word that belongs in each sentence.

1. Ms. Bryant is _____ about her students' feelings.
   **inception**    **perceptive**    **participate**
2. To ensure pick-up, the trash _____ was placed in the driveway.
   **conception**    **reception**    **receptacle**
3. Maria's _____ about what a vacation should be led to disappointment.
   **precipitous**    **preconceptions**    **receivables**
4. Michael was the proud _____ of the most valuable player award.
   **recipient**    **reception**    **receptor**
5. After the police officer heard all the facts, there was a _____ change in his tone.
   **conceivable**    **perceptible**    **precipice**
6. Dave has been with the youth sports program since its _____.
   **precept**    **inception**    **imperceptible**
7. Thanks to the efforts of many villagers, the _____ racial tension was diffused.
   **deceivable**    **participial**    **incipient**
8. After five undefeated seasons, it was _____ to the swim team to lose an event.
   **inconceivable**    **preconceived**    **precipitation**
9. The visiting dignitary from the troubled nation received a warm _____.
   **deception**    **reception**    **conception**
10. Ned liked challenges, but the _____ slopes facing him subdued his zeal to climb.
    **precipitous**    **precipitation**    **receptacle**

**B.** Write the words you circled in Exercise A. Underline the word roots and write the definition of the words.

_____
_____
_____
_____
_____
_____

**10** Vocabulary Practice 10: Word Roots        © Prentice-Hall, Inc.

Name _____  Date _____

# Vocabulary Practice 11: Word Roots

**Word Roots:** *-cad-, -cas-, -cid-*

    A **word root** forms the basic part of all words and gives the word its primary meaning. Knowing the meaning of a word root can help you determine the meaning of the whole word.

    The word roots *-cad-, -cas-,* and *-cid-* all mean "fall." The word *incidence* means "an act of falling upon" or "affecting"; "an occurrence."

**A.** Underline the word in each sentence with a root that means "fall."

1. Occasional get-togethers give people a chance to catch up with each other.
2. The driving safety board is addressing the high casualty rate among teenagers.
3. William's dental appointment coincided with errands he had planned in the city.
4. Decadent buildings in our city have been restored to their original beauty.
5. The students' books cascaded to the floor when they collided in the hall.
6. "Occidental" is used to refer to the world west of Asia.
7. Incidental expenses can add up to large amounts of money quickly.
8. The mortician worked with the cadaver and made notes for the autopsy.
9. The horses' training in cadent maneuvers was demonstrated by the equestrians.
10. Tim's and Lindsay's appointments in the city hall were a fortuitous coincidence.

**B.** Write the underlined words from Exercise A with their definitions.

_____  1. having inflection or rhythm in tone

_____  2. deteriorated

_____  3. fell or poured in a succession of stages

_____  4. an accidental occurrence of events

_____  5. a person or thing lost, injured, or destroyed

_____  6. happening infrequently

_____  7. resembling a dead body

_____  8. occurred simultaneously

_____  9. western

_____  10. unplanned

**C.** Write as many forms of the underlined words as you can. Then write a brief definition of each word.

_____
_____
_____
_____
_____

© Prentice-Hall, Inc.

Name _____   Date _____

# Vocabulary Practice 12: Word Roots

**Word Roots:** *-aug-* or *-aux-*, *-cre-*, *-cres-*, *-cret-*

A **word root** forms the basic part of all words and gives the word its primary meaning. If you know the meaning of a root form, you can determine the meaning of the whole word.

The word roots *-aug-* or *-aux-*, *-cre-*, *-cres-*, and *-cret-* all mean "grow." The word *increase* means "to make or become greater in size, amount, or degree."

**A.** Each boldface word is written in a phrase that is a clue to the word's meaning. Write the boldface word and its definition.

**augment** funds           **incremental** raises       **auxiliary** firemen
**crescent** moon           played **crescendo**         **augur** a tornado
**augmentative** word       small **increments**         room **augmentation**
**accretion** of sand and gravel

1. _____
2. _____
3. _____
4. _____
5. _____
6. _____
7. _____
8. _____
9. _____
10. _____

**B.** Write a short passage using five of the boldface words from Exercise A. Use the following passage beginning or your own topic sentence. Underline the boldface words you use.

The woman needed a break from sitting at her small, dimly lighted desk. She stood and walked to the dingy window, encrusted with soot and grime from the traffic below.

_____
_____
_____
_____
_____
_____
_____

**12** Vocabulary Practice 12: Word Roots                           © Prentice-Hall, Inc.

Name _____  Date _____

# Vocabulary Practice 13: Word Roots

## Word Roots: Latin and Greek Roots

Many English words have Latin and Greek roots. Knowing the meanings of roots will help you to determine the meanings of unfamiliar words.

**A.** Identify the two words in each sentence with different roots, but similar meanings. Underline the words. Then, write the root meanings and the definitions of both words. Use a dictionary, if necessary.

1. Because it was an aquatic animal, the seal quickly became dangerously dehydrated on dry land. _____
   _____

2. The passionate anglophile was enamored by anything related to the British royal family.
   _____
   _____

3. The entire population turned out to vote for a democratic government. _____
   _____

4. After his long walk, the pedestrian went to a podiatrist to heal his sore feet. _____
   _____

5. The extremely sensitive patient needed more anesthetic to block the pain. _____
   _____

6. The dentist referred the man to an orthodontist to have his teeth aligned. _____
   _____

7. The young woman consulted an orthopedist to correct her bent posture. _____
   _____

8. The asteroid was so far from Earth that it appeared fixed in the sky and seemed to form part of a constellation. _____
   _____

9. The spectators wished they had a telescope to see the distant stage. _____
   _____

10. The photographer needed better illumination to avoid shadows in the pictures. _____
    _____

11. The man peered intently through the binoculars, not knowing that what he was seeing was merely an optical illusion. _____
    _____

12. The action of the powerful antibiotic drained any animation from the boy's face. _____
    _____

© Prentice-Hall, Inc.

# Vocabulary Practice 13: Word Roots

13. The dedicated scientist found it incredible that anyone could be ignorant of the workings of a computer. _____

14. The warmth of the visitor's cordial invitation was not lost on the cardiac patient, who had felt depressed and isolated since his heart attack. _____

15. The anthropologist explained that hominids walk on two feet rather than four. _____

16. Neophyte investors do not always recognize that online trading is a jarring innovation for long-time brokers in this staid field. _____

17. The brightly colored posters of a busy metropolis glamorized urban life. _____

18. The actress's autograph was encased in a silver frame inscribed with her initials. _____

19. The research biologist labored around the clock to find a cure. _____

20. The sonorous triangle rang out in the middle of the symphony. _____

**B.** Prepare this chart of roots, prefixes, and suffixes. Begin by listing the words you underlined in Exercise A. Write the prefixes and suffixes in the labeled columns. Then, read the sentences in Exercise A again to find other words with different roots and write those roots, prefixes, and suffixes in the chart. Finally, use the dictionary to add as many words as you can with the same roots. You will have a detailed chart to explain unfamiliar words when you read!

| Words | Roots and Their Meanings | Prefixes | Suffixes |
|---|---|---|---|
|  |  |  |  |
|  |  |  |  |
|  |  |  |  |
|  |  |  |  |
|  |  |  |  |
|  |  |  |  |
|  |  |  |  |
|  |  |  |  |
|  |  |  |  |
|  |  |  |  |
|  |  |  |  |

Name _____  Date _____

# Vocabulary Practice 14: Synonyms

A **synonym** is a word with the same or nearly the same meaning as another word.

**Example:** The word *diverse* is a synonym for the word *multifarious*.

**A.** Underline the word in each sentence that is a synonym for the boldface word. Then, write a brief definition for the boldface word. Use a dictionary, as necessary.

1. Kate is greatly admired because she devotes her time to altruistic causes.
   **charitable** _____

2. After hours of continuous enemy fire, the beleaguered troops surrendered to the Union army.
   **attacked** _____

3. The agency was contacted to investigate the clandestine activities of the spy.
   **furtive** _____

4. Amanda took copious notes, hoping to ensure a passing grade on the final exam.
   **extensive** _____

5. When she began writing her paper, Lisa had a dearth of research on her topic.
   **scarcity** _____

6. It was difficult to imagine Edward, a voluble man, listening while others voiced their opinions.
   **verbose** _____

7. The interior decorator called the lamp an egregious example of bad taste.
   **glaring** _____

8. Because of poor organization, Ted's financial records appeared to be spurious.
   **deceptive** _____

9. When consumed, even a small amount of poisonous substance can be virulent.
   **lethal** _____

10. Only a portion of the author's voluminous correspondence has been published.
    **profuse** _____

**B.** On other paper, write as many synonyms as you can for each word. Use a thesaurus, as necessary.

1. **charitable**
2. **attacked**
3. **furtive**
4. **extensive**
5. **insufficient**
6. **verbose**
7. **glaring**
8. **deceptive**
9. **lethal**
10. **profuse**

© Prentice-Hall, Inc.

Name _____  Date _____

# Vocabulary Practice 15: Synonyms

A **synonym** is a word with the same or nearly the same meaning as another word.

**Example:** The word *parity* is a synonym for *equality*.

**A.** Circle the word that is *not* a synonym for the boldface word.

1. **extolled**    a) praised    b) hailed    c) criticized    d) lauded
2. **enthralled**    a) captivated    b) mesmerized    c) thrilled    d) exhausted
3. **repudiated**    a) disavowed    b) rejected    c) embraced    d) disclaimed
4. **regimen**    a) system    b) location    c) routine    d) formula
5. **appeased**    a) inspired    b) satisfied    c) placated    d) gratified
6. **inscrutable**    a) mysterious    b) perplexing    c) strange    d) understandable
7. **delectable**    a) delicious    b) savory    c) flavorless    d) pleasing
8. **laconic**    a) concise    b) rambling    c) terse    d) curt
9. **elucidate**    a) emulate    b) explain    c) clarify    d) interpret
10. **acrimonious**    a) caustic    b) angry    c) amiable    d) bitter

**B.** Write the boldface words from Exercise A in these sentences.

1. Partisan committee members were not _____ by the president's concessions.
2. The music critic _____ the natural ability and talent of the young prodigy.
3. A new architect _____ the designs of Frank Lloyd Wright in favor of a contemporary designer.
4. The kindergarten children were absolutely _____ with the mystifying magic tricks performed by the magician.
5. Louis embarked on a strict _____ of exercise that included grueling hours at the gym.
6. The debate began in a cordial manner, but it quickly degenerated into an _____ dispute.
7. Although the main entree was tasteless, the desserts at the restaurant were _____.
8. Because many students in the class misunderstood the poem, Ms. Cisneros tried to _____ the meaning.
9. The _____ writing of Ernest Hemingway was in sharp contrast to the more verbose writers of the 1920s.
10. As the poet's works became darker and more _____ , her fans found her verses difficult to understand.

Name _____   Date _____

# Vocabulary Practice 16: Synonyms

A **synonym** is a word with the same or nearly the same meaning as another word.

**Example:** The word *solace* is a synonym for *consolation*.

**A.** In these synonym analogies, circle the letter of the word pair that completes the analogy.

1. ADVOCATE:DEFENDER::_____
    a. supporter:candidate
    b. campaign:strategies
    c. accolade:award
    d. eulogy:death
    e. fledgling:experienced

2. GARISH:GAUDY::_____
    a. showy:reserved
    b. misery:tragedy
    c. morbid:cemeteries
    d. beautiful:ugly
    e. haughty:arrogant

3. MOTLEY:SPOTTED::_____
    a. maniacal:sane
    b. superstitious:believable
    c. destructive:building
    d. multifarious:diverse
    e. flattened:buoyed

4. INNOCUOUS:HARMLESS::_____
    a. innocent:harmful
    b. knotty:grainy
    c. intractable:unruly
    d. loyal:derisive
    e. jealous:ruinous

5. QUERULOUS:TESTY::_____
    a. judicious:reasonable
    b. courtly:king
    c. judgmental:attentive
    d. fickle:consistent
    e. mature:feasible

6. HISTRIONIC:MELODRAMATIC::_____
    a. greedy:deceptive
    b. raucous:harsh
    c. dramatic:coach
    d. legible:written
    e. tragedy:miserable

7. POROUS:PERMEABLE::_____
    a. compliment:insult
    b. sponge:moisture
    c. dew:meadow
    d. problematic:preventative
    e. pliable:limber

8. HIATUS:PAUSE::_____
    a. manners:polite
    b. ballerina:dancer
    c. precursor:forerunner
    d. quarantine:patient
    e. language:orator

9. ANOMALY:ABNORMALITY::_____
    a. language:message
    b. entertainer:script
    c. educator:lecturer
    d. progeny:descendant
    e. cola:beverage

10. PEJORATIVE:DEGRADING::_____
    a. cohesive:divisive
    b. proud:flawed
    c. surly:rude
    d. complex:problem
    e. humble:vain

**B.** Write a word that completes these synonym analogies.

1. ADROIT:SKILLFUL::BOORISH: _____

2. CACOPHONOUS:DISCORDANT::CHERUBIC: _____

3. GUZZLE:GULP::EXPEDITE: _____

4. LETHARGY:IDLENESS::LEVITY: _____

5. INTERCEDE:INTERVENE::JETTISON: _____

Name _____  Date _____

# Vocabulary Practice 17: Antonyms

An **antonym** is a word that is opposite in meaning to another word.

**Example:** The word *ignorance* is an antonym for the word *intelligence*.

**A.** Write two words from the list that are antonyms for each boldface word. Then, write a sentence using the boldface word.

| flattering | benevolent | enlighten | regularity | clarify |
| jovial | emotional | significant | favorable | obtuse |
| appease | normality | penetrable | genial | accessible |
| sensitive | virtuous | impressive | compliment | naive |

1. **disoblige** _____ _____
   _____

2. **disputatious** _____ _____
   _____

3. **anomaly** _____ _____
   _____

4. **obfuscate** _____ _____
   _____

5. **impervious** _____ _____
   _____

6. **disaffected** _____ _____
   _____

7. **nefarious** _____ _____
   _____

8. **paltry** _____ _____
   _____

9. **percipient** _____ _____
   _____

10. **pejorative** _____ _____
    _____

**B.** Write brief meanings for these words, and then list two antonyms for each boldface word. Use a dictionary or thesaurus, if necessary.

1. **enervate** _____

2. **dither** _____

3. **chary** _____

4. **elegiac** _____

5. **quixotic** _____

Name _____  Date _____

# Vocabulary Practice 18: Antonyms

An **antonym** is a word that is opposite in meaning to another word.

**Example:** The word *odious* is an antonym for *admirable*.

**A.** Underline the word in each sentence that is an antonym for the boldface word. Then, write another antonym for the boldface word.

1. The acuity of the impressive keynote speaker was in sharp contrast to the **dullness** of the subsequent lecturers. _____

2. One ruler's bellicose nature and the other's **peaceful** tactics were well publicized. _____

3. The movie star's commodious closet overshadowed her **cramped** dressing room. _____

4. The captain's unusually irascible nature alarmed the **docile** first mate.

5. Mr. Johnson's **tyranny** as a manager led to anarchy when his subordinates threatened to strike. _____

6. The **reserved** student was contemptuous of the professor's vivacious delivery. _____

7. The **simple** facade contrasted with the florid interior decoration. _____

8. Although she was meticulous about spelling, the editor was **haphazard** in her use of correct punctuation. _____

9. The role of a garrulous sales associate stretched the talents of the **laconic** actor. _____

10. Scrooge's saturnine disposition became **cheerful** after the spectral visitation. _____

**B.** Write as many antonyms as you can for the boldface words. Then, write a sentence using each boldface word and its antonym.

1. **tenuous** _____

2. **dispassionate** _____

3. **enigmatic** _____

4. **impetuous** _____

5. **laxity** _____

© Prentice-Hall, Inc.

Name _____   Date _____

# Vocabulary Practice 19: Antonyms

An **antonym** is a word that is opposite in meaning to another word.

**Example:** The word *evasive* is an antonym for *straightforward*.

**A.** In these antonym analogies, circle the letter of the pair of words that completes the analogy.

1. IMPROVIDENT:THOUGHTFUL::_____
   a. believable:dramatic
   b. caring:concerned
   c. pathetic:profitable
   d. quiet:pensive
   e. amorphous:shaped

2. APATHY:CONCERN::_____
   a. linguist:nouns
   b. botany:science
   c. duress:threat
   d. adherent:doubter
   e. fraud:hoax

3. CEASE:BEGIN::_____
   a. augment:extent
   b. buttress:support
   c. aggrandize:decrease
   d. cajole:flatter
   e. examine:canvass

4. BOISTEROUS:QUIET::_____
   a. affluent:abundant
   b. burly:brawny
   c. insensitive:callous
   d. baleful:harmless
   e. blatant:obvious

5. CALLOW:EXPERIENCED::_____
   a. brusque:abrupt
   b. censorious:uncritical
   c. civil:polite
   d. accomplished:consummate
   e. secret:covert

6. CONTENTIOUS:AGREEABLE::_____
   a. garrulous:talkative
   b. incredulous:unbelievable
   c. imposing:grand
   d. flawless:impeccable
   e. impromptu:rehearsed

7. DESOLATE:HOPEFUL::_____
   a. irrevocable:irreversible
   b. unsatisfied:insatiable
   c. lurid:sensational
   d. pleased:discontent
   e. mandatory:required

8. EXTRICATE:ENTANGLE::_____
   a. adhere:cling
   b. tangle:confuse
   c. disclose:harbor
   d. aggrieve:distress
   e. atrophy:wither

9. INSIPID:EXCITING::_____
   a. habitual:occasional
   b. tasteful:decorous
   c. deformed:disfigured
   d. paltry:worthless
   e. remote:distant

10. KUDOS:CRITICISM::_____
    a. clamor:noise
    b. nadir:pinnacle
    c. shame:chagrin
    d. obesity:corpulence
    e. deluge:water

**B.** Write a word that completes these analogies.

1. COMPLIMENT:INSULT::RESTIVE: _____

2. VISIBLE:CONCEALED::DELETERIOUS: _____

3. MALADROIT:SKILLED::METICULOUS: _____

4. MALLEABLE:RIGID::NOXIOUS: _____

5. ELONGATE:PROTRACT::OSTRACIZE: _____

Name _____  Date _____

# Vocabulary Practice 20: Synonym and Antonym Review

A **synonym** is a word with the same or nearly the same meaning as another word. An **antonym** is a word that is opposite in meaning to another word.

**Examples:** A synonym for *concise* is *brief*. An antonym for *concise* is *lengthy*.

**A.** Write a synonym and an antonym for the italicized word in each sentence.

1. The *brevity* of Kenneth's essay compared favorably to Nancy's lengthy one.
   **synonym:** _____ **antonym:** _____

2. For his war crimes, the *nefarious* dictator was sentenced to prison.
   **synonym:** _____ **antonym:** _____

3. This year, the fundraisers received more than the *paltry* donations of last year.
   **synonym:** _____ **antonym:** _____

4. Dennis' *malevolent* stare frightened the cat who scurried under the porch.
   **synonym:** _____ **antonym:** _____

5. A local manufacturer received the *dubious* honor of being the state's major polluter.
   **synonym:** _____ **antonym:** _____

6. It took several minutes for the stunt man to *extricate* himself from the trunk.
   **synonym:** _____ **antonym:** _____

7. Some candidates prepared their remarks and others speak *extemporaneously*.
   **synonym:** _____ **antonym:** _____

8. An *amorphous* air mass spread over the sky just minutes before the storm began.
   **synonym:** _____ **antonym:** _____

9. Lyle's research document included *copious* references to scholarly works.
   **synonym:** _____ **antonym:** _____

10. Because of his *altruistic* nature, Nicholas contributed to many causes.
    **synonym:** _____ **antonym:** _____

11. With a *dearth* of information on her thesis topic, Anita changed the theme.
    **synonym:** _____ **antonym:** _____

12. Dave *repudiated* the trumped-up charges brought against him by a neighbor.
    **synonym:** _____ **antonym:** _____

13. Mr. Cousous, a master chef, demonstrated recipes for his *delectable* pastries.
    **synonym:** _____ **antonym:** _____

14. Regrettably, mediation efforts degenerated into an *acrimonious* dispute.
    **synonym:** _____ **antonym:** _____

15. Mr. Roberts *elucidated* the meaning of the author's convoluted essay.
    **synonym:** _____ **antonym:** _____

**B.** On other paper, rewrite the sentences in Exercise A using either the synonym or the antonym for the boldface word.

© Prentice-Hall, Inc.

Name _____  Date _____

# Vocabulary Practice 21: Analogies

An **analogy** shows a relationship, or makes a comparison, between two pairs of words. In an analogy, the relationship between the words in the first pair is compared to the relationship of the words in the second pair.

**Example:** One type of relationship is a *function* relationship. RUDDER:STEER::ANCHOR:STABILIZE

**Example:** One type of relationship is a *cause-effect* relationship.
CARELESSNESS:MISTAKES::HURRICANE:DESTRUCTION

**A.** Think about the relationship between the words in the first pair. Circle the letter before the pair of words that completes the analogy.

1. INJURY:SCAR::_____
   a. monument:war
   b. largess:poverty
   c. juncture:seam
   d. illness:temperature
   e. crash:dent

2. DEATH:INTERMENT::_____
   a. beach:swimming
   b. invention:invent
   c. laboratory:experiment
   d. fatigue:sleep
   e. theory:formulate

3. TARP:COVER::_____
   a. hawk:beak
   b. shell:crab
   c. queen:crown
   d. hunter:firearm
   e. wolf:den

4. BOREDOM:YAWN::_____
   a. sleep:recline
   b. depression:recession
   c. surprise:smile
   d. unhappiness:pout
   e. happiness:joy

5. MICROSCOPE:MAGNIFY::_____
   a. legislature:debate
   b. playground:slide
   c. crutch:support
   d. computer:screen
   e. eulogy:speech

6. CLOUD:RAIN::_____
   a. salad:lettuce
   b. friendship:secrets
   c. aperture:camera
   d. burn:pain
   e. buttress:support

7. SATISFACTION:GRATITUDE::_____
   a. precipice:cliff
   b. joke:ridicule
   c. timidity:nervousness
   d. victory:heroes
   e. enthusiasm:entertainment

8. MICROPHONE:AMPLIFY::_____
   a. scissors:sewing
   b. siren:warning
   c. stopwatch:running
   d. helicopter:rescue
   e. automobile:pleasure

9. HAMMER:POUND::_____
   a. stethoscope:listen
   b. scale:reduce
   c. drill:bore
   d. bandage:wound
   e. eraser:mistake

10. PURSUIT:CAPTURE::_____
    a. abdicate:flee
    b. disband:unite
    c. dissuade:convince
    d. embroil:involve
    e. persuasion:agreement

**B.** Write a pair of words with the same relationship as the given pair.

1. PROBLEM:ANXIETY:: _____
2. POLLUTION:ENVIRONMENT:: _____
3. PARDON:FREEDOM:: _____
4. CRANE:DEMOLITION:: _____
5. WHISPERING:TALKING:: _____

22  Vocabulary Practice 21: Analogies                © Prentice-Hall, Inc.

Name _____  Date _____

# Vocabulary Practice 22: Analogies

An **analogy** shows a relationship, or makes a comparison, between two pairs of words. In an analogy, the relationship between the words in the first pair is compared to the relationship of the words in the second pair.

**Example:** One type of analogy expresses a *part to whole* or *part of* relationship. In WOLF:PACK::COW:HERD, "wolf" is part of "pack," and "cow" is part of "herd."

**Example:** Another analogy type shows a *type of* relationship. In NEON:GAS::QUARTZ:MINERAL, "neon" is a type of "gas," and "quartz" is a type of "mineral."

**A.** Circle the letter before the pair of words that completes the analogy.

1. LEGEND:MAP::_____
   a. event:plot
   b. portrait:camera
   c. orbit:satellite
   d. bandage:wound
   e. knoll:mound

2. SILK:FABRIC::_____
   a. worm:insect
   b. weaving:clothing
   c. sonnet:poem
   d. reflection:appearance
   e. antelope:grasslands

3. MASON:CRAFTSMAN::_____
   a. hammer:nail
   b. structure:building
   c. stethoscope:physician
   d. odometer:gauge
   e. volume:anthology

4. VARIABLE:EQUATION::_____
   a. remnant:fabric
   b. lever:pulley
   c. object:phrase
   d. number:series
   e. chronological:summary

5. SPONDEE:METER::_____
   a. sequoia:tree
   b. harvest:autumn
   c. telephone:communication
   d. keypad:computer
   e. entry:collaboration

6. METAL:ALLOY::_____
   a. shafts:mine
   b. mining:ore
   c. wheat:chaff
   d. sonata:aria
   e. ingredients:recipe

7. PARALLEL:CIRCUIT::_____
   a. technology:history
   b. fluorine:element
   c. statement:contract
   d. library:card catalog
   e. receipt:transaction

8. STANZA:POEM::_____
   a. elevator:shaft
   b. chord:octave
   c. paragraph:article
   d. stairs:risers
   e. research:citations

9. PREMISE:ARGUMENT::_____
   a. recruits:army
   b. estimate:extrapolation
   c. brick:mortar
   d. evidence:case
   e. roof:shingles

10. SKYSCRAPER:BUILDING::_____
    a. exhaust:pollution
    b. mesa:horizon
    c. beach:dunes
    d. sound:volume
    e. uniform:nurse

**B.** On another piece of paper, write an analogy for each of these types of word relationships: "part to whole," "part of," and "type of."

© Prentice-Hall, Inc.                    Vocabulary Practice 22: Analogies  23

Name _____   Date _____

# Vocabulary Practice 23: Analogies

An **analogy** shows a relationship, or makes a comparison, between two pairs of words. In an analogy, the relationship between the words in the first pair is compared to the relationship of words in the second pair.

**A.** You have studied several types of analogies, including *synonyms, antonyms, function, cause-effect, part to whole, part of,* and *type of* relationships. Complete these analogies by choosing the word pair that has the same relationship as the first pair.

1. INTANGIBLE:ABSTRACT:: _____
   a. nebulous:tenuous
   b. similar:opposite
   c. vacuous:vapid
   d. sympathetic:antagonistic
   e. amorphous:impalpable

2. SHIELD:DEFLECT:: _____
   a. steer:harness
   b. walks:boot
   c. sneaker:sprint
   d. dictionary:define
   e. yoke:plod

3. NOVICE:SAGE:: _____
   a. inane:incoherent
   b. incongruent:parallel
   c. indigenous:alien
   d. intellectual:emotional
   e. treacherous:dangerous

4. AVAIRY:ZOO:: _____
   a. birdhouse:garden
   b. apiary:center
   c. fence:ranch
   d. memory:cortex
   e. cell:prison

5. TORNADO:DESTRUCTION:: _____
   a. mentor:instruction
   b. virus:illness
   c. government:defiance
   d. mug:drink
   e. e-mail:communication

6. CANOPY:SHELTER:: _____
   a. bliss:joy
   b. music:classical
   c. garbage:compost
   d. congestion:traffic
   e. tulip:flower

7. VORACIOUS:RAVENOUS:: _____
   a. decent:decrepit
   b. envious:resentful
   c. chaotic:confused
   d. gluttonous:famished
   e. ruinous:constructive

8. ISLAND:ARCHIPELAGO:: _____
   a. worker:union
   b. sphincter:esophagus
   c. mountain:plains
   d. lid:container
   e. foyer:hearth

9. RESERVED:VIVACIOUS:: _____
   a. reflective: impulsive
   b. compulsive:obsessive
   c. passive:indifferent
   d. prospective:futuristic
   e. withered:atrophied

10. SCHOOLING:KNOWLEDGE:: _____
    a. writing:composition
    b. repetition:habit
    c. disease:analgesic
    d. water:satiation
    e. wheel:rotation

**B.** Write a different pair of words to complete each analogy in Exercise A.

1. _____
2. _____
3. _____
4. _____
5. _____

6. _____
7. _____
8. _____
9. _____
10. _____

Name _____  Date _____

# Vocabulary Practice 24: Connotations and Denotations

A **connotation** is the implied or suggested meaning of a word or phrase. It is different from the **denotation**, or dictionary definition. Connotations convey implied meanings—positive, neutral, or negative—depending on the text.

**Example:** *Bashful* and *diffident* describe a person afraid to put himself or herself forward. *Bashful* describes someone who is uncomfortable around people, while *diffident* describes someone hesitant to draw attention because of a lack of confidence.

**A.** Complete the sentences with two of the given words. Some words require different endings. Write a sentence using the remaining word to convey its connotation.

1. Words that connote "something unending" are *infinite*, *eternal*, and *interminable*.

   a. The speaker's _____ speech made the moderator wish she had set a timer.

   b. The couple vowed _____ love even though their families kept them apart.

   c. _____

2. Words that connote "ways of speaking" are *mutter*, *drone*, and *ramble*.

   a. The chairperson _____ on about the importance of protocol during meetings.

   b. The cashier _____ about inconsiderate customers as she gave the man his change.

   c. _____

3. Words that connote "degrees of happiness" are *glad*, *euphoric*, and *content*.

   a. The medical student was _____ upon learning she got her first-choice hospital for residency.

   b. The plaintiff was genuinely _____ with the settlement he had hoped to receive.

   c. _____

4. Words that connote "degrees of firmness" are i*mmovable*, *inelastic*, and *inflexible*.

   a. The senator was _____ in his position about the environmental bill he created.

   b. Grandpa is _____ when people try to persuade him to give up his chocoholic diet.

   c. _____

5. Words that connote "degrees of fullness" are *saturated*, *engorged*, and *replete*.

   a. The ground was _____ after the heavy spring rains that lasted several days.

   b. The catered dinner was _____ with a variety of imported delicacies.

   c. _____

**B.** On another piece of paper, write another word for each set of connotations in Exercise A.

Name _____  Date _____

# Vocabulary Practice 25: Connotations and Denotations

A **connotation** is the implied or suggested meaning of a word or phrase. It is different from the **denotation**, or dictionary definition.

**Example:** The denotation for *proud* is "feeling a reasonable amount of self-esteem." There are many connotations for *proud*.

**A.** Complete each sentence with a word from the list to convey the connotation of *proud*.

**arrogant, exalted, haughty, lordly, insolent, overbearing, supercilious, spirited, disdainful, conceited, immodest, prideful, superior, condescending, patronizing, snobbish, snooty, inflated, swollen, snippy, cocky, vainglorious, uppity, assuming, pompous, boastful**

1. Jenny had been a quiet, unassuming young lady until she won the state spelling bee; then the award went to her head. She became _____, bragging to everyone about her intelligence.

2. Most employees were happy about the insurance executive's meteoric rise within the corporation, but they were not pleased when he became _____ as a result of his promotions.

3. Because Lord Wexler had been born into an aristocratic family, he adopted a rather _____ attitude toward those he thought "common."

4. Although the food was delicious, our evening at the famous five-star restaurant was tainted by the service of the rude, _____ waiter.

5. After winning the gold medal at the Olympics and signing endorsements contracts, the young athlete became _____ to the friends she left behind.

**B.** Choose one of the sentences in Exercise A to begin a paragraph. Add two or three sentences, using words from the list in Exercise A. Include details or other information to convey the appropriate connotations of the words you use.

_____
_____
_____
_____
_____
_____
_____
_____
_____
_____

Name _____   Date _____

# Vocabulary Practice 26: Connotations and Denotations

A **connotation** is the implied or suggested meaning of a word or phrase. It is different from the **denotation**, or dictionary definition. Connotations convey positive, neutral, or negative feelings.

**Example:** The words *autocratic* and *authoritative* have roughly the same denotative meaning "giving orders," but different connotations. *Authoritative* connotes "assertiveness," which may be positive or neutral, while *autocratic* connotes "domination," which is a negative connotation.

**A.** Write the words in each set under one of the headings to classify their connotations. Some words may be listed in two columns. You will need another piece of paper.

1. stingy, thrifty, economical, frugal, parsimonious, miserly
2. tenacious, bulldogged, firm, rigid, persistent, stubborn
3. secretive, sly, furtive, surreptitious, sneaky, clandestine
4. desire, covet, wish, crave, yearn, need
5. aged, venerable, old, ancient, hoary, antiquated

| Positive | Neutral | Negative |
|---|---|---|
| _____ | _____ | _____ |
| _____ | _____ | _____ |
| _____ | _____ | _____ |
| _____ | _____ | _____ |
| _____ | _____ | _____ |
| _____ | _____ | _____ |
| _____ | _____ | _____ |

**B.** The words in each pair have similar denotations, but very different connotations. Write the definition for each word. Then choose one word in each pair and write a sentence to convey its connotation.

1. **obedient** and **obsequious** _____

2. **gigantic** and **monstrous** _____

3. **lasting** and **interminable** _____

4. **enthusiasm** and **mania** _____

5. **spontaneous** and **impulsive** _____

© Prentice-Hall, Inc.                    Vocabulary Practice 26: Connotations and Denotations  **27**

Name _____  Date _____

# Vocabulary Practice 27: Commonly Misused Words

Having a good vocabulary demands skillful use of the right words in speaking and writing. Many words and phrases cause confusion because their meanings are not understood or because the words sound alike.

**Example:** The words *imply* and *infer* often cause confusion. *Imply* means "to suggest or state directly." *Infer* means "to draw conclusions from information."

**A.** Write a brief definition for each boldface word.

1. **access** and **excess** _____
2. **adapted to** and **adapted from** _____
3. **allude** and **elude** _____
4. **amount** and **number** _____
5. **ceremonial** and **ceremonious** _____
6. **accede** and **concede** _____
7. **adverse** and **averse** _____
8. **aggravate** and **irritate** _____
9. **allusion** and **reference** _____
10. **intercede** and **intercept** _____

**B.** Choose a word from each pair of words in Exercise A to complete the corresponding numbered sentences below. Some words require different endings.

1. _____ to the library's rare collections room was limited to doctoral students.
2. The drama club's play was _____ a novel written by their English teacher.
3. In his monthly address, the mayor _____ to an increase in taxes next year.
4. An advertising special doubled the _____ of customers last week.
5. Ornate, _____ robes worn by the crown prince were displayed in a glass case.
6. The chess champion did _____ that he was concerned about his opponent's skill.
7. Children entering the country were given medicine, which caused _____ reactions.
8. Intense heat and humidity seemed to _____ Marita's case of poison ivy.
9. In an _____ to the familiar story, the main character was Jonah.
10. Negotiations were unsuccessful until mediators _____ for the employees.

**C.** Write sentences for four words not used in Exercise B.

_____
_____
_____
_____

28  Vocabulary Practice 27: Commonly Misused Words                © Prentice-Hall, Inc.

Name _____   Date _____

# Vocabulary Practice 28: Commonly Misused Words

Having a good vocabulary demands skillful use of the right words in speaking and writing. Many words and phrases cause confusion because their meanings are not understood or because the words sound alike.

**Example:** The words *ability* and *capacity* are often used incorrectly. The word *ability* means "skill," while the word *capacity* means "aptitude."

**A.** Write the boldface words in the pairs of sentences.

1. **comprised, composed**

    Approximately ten percent of our military forces is _____ of women.

    A committee _____ of four senators was convened for the hearing.

2. **continual, continuous, contiguous**

    The _____ buzz of the computer made the worker sleepy.

    The _____ row of townhouses was built in a fashionable part of town.

    During the war, the _____ threat of an air attack made Londoners uneasy.

3. **cynical, skeptical**

    John was _____ about buying a used car from the enthusiastic salesman.

    The disgruntled and _____ employees did not believe the promises of the new manager.

4. **definite, definitive**

    The principal set _____ standards for acceptable behavior.

    The author researched and wrote the _____ book on the Kennedy assassination.

5. **delusion, illusion**

    Although he was overweight, Jim had created the _____ of being fit and trim.

    Regrettably, most people who have a _____ of becoming millionaires are disappointed.

**B.** Write the definitions of the boldface words.

1. **egoism** _____

    **egotism** _____

2. **eliminate** _____

    **illuminate** _____

3. **enhance** _____

    **improve** _____

4. **extrinsic** _____

    **intrinsic** _____

5. **tenable** _____

    **tenuous** _____

Name _____  Date _____

# Vocabulary Practice 29: Commonly Misused Words

Having a good vocabulary demands skillful use of the right words in speaking and writing. Many words and phrases cause confusion because their meanings are not understood or because the words sound alike.

**Example:** The words *adverse* and *averse* are often used incorrectly. The word *adverse* means "unfavorable," while the word *averse* means "reluctant."

**A.** Write the boldface word pairs in the correct order in each sentence.

1. Although I had _____ met the representative at a local fundraiser, we were _____ introduced by the campaign manager. **formerly, formally**

2. We purchased the lush shrubbery within the _____ of a tight budget and planted the beautiful bushes along the _____ of the property. **parameter, perimeter**

3. Juan was told that a college degree is a _____ of the job, and a _____ of the job is a company car for him to drive. **perquisite, prerequisite**

4. From the English professor's _____, his students were _____ English scholars. **perspective, prospective**

5. When the businessman donated money to the boys club, the _____ boosted his reputation; unfortunately, some of his personal life gave him _____. **publicity, notoriety**

**B.** Write the word that completes the sentence. Then, write a sentence using the other word in each pair.

1. When the president injured his knee, an _____ orthopedic surgeon was summoned.
   **imminent, eminent**
   _____

2. Crowds cheered when the defense _____ the pass and ran for the touchdown.
   **interceded, intercepted**
   _____

3. History books recount the _____ of people because of their religious beliefs.
   **prosecution, persecution**
   _____

4. Some of my favorite _____ are from Emily Dickinson's poetry.
   **quotes, quotations**
   _____

5. Mr. Todd was _____ to leave his young children with the inexperienced baby sitter.
   **reluctant, reticent**
   _____

30 Vocabulary Practice 29: Commonly Misused Words

Name _____ Date _____

# Vocabulary Practice 30: Specialized Vocabulary

Computers are used by almost everyone today. It is necessary to be familiar with computer technology when working with computers or when conversing about computer-related work.

**A.** Match each computer-related term with its meaning. Write the letter of the definition before the word.

1. ___ **cursor**
2. ___ **database**
3. ___ **documentation**
4. ___ **graphics**
5. ___ **instructions**
6. ___ **interactive**
7. ___ **network**
8. ___ **memory**
9. ___ **telecommunications**
10. ___ **virus**

a. a system of computers, terminals, and databases connected by communications lines
b. a code that tells a computer to perform a particular operation
c. of or relating to a two-way electronic communication system
d. the storage capacity of a computer or disk
e. a large collection of data organized especially for rapid search and retrieval
f. communication by electronic means, for example, through computers
g. the printed instructions, information, and comments for using a particular piece or system of hardware or software
h. a visual cue on a video display that indicates position
i. a computer program, usually hidden inside another program, that causes damage
j. visual display of text or images

**B.** Write the computer term from Exercise A that completes each sentence.

1. The _____ blinked rapidly, awaiting the next command from its operator.
2. Linc referred to the _____ to find out how to input the data.
3. As more people work at home, reliable _____ becomes increasingly important.
4. The expanded _____ allowed all the departments to share e-mail.
5. The huge _____ contained information on all the company's customers.
6. The computer executed the program according to the _____ Mei had written.
7. The _____ on the old computer seemed grainy and disjointed.
8. Shawna discovered the _____ before it damaged any of the files.
9. The _____ web site allowed Hector to order online.
10. When Cam's computer began to run out of _____, he looked at other options.

**C.** Use a dictionary or computer resource to write the definitions of these computer terms.

1. **programming language** _____
2. **input** _____
3. **binary** _____
4. **byte** _____
5. **spreadsheet** _____

Name _____ Date _____

# Vocabulary Practice 31: Specialized Vocabulary

Many words and phrases we use in everyday conversation are from the lexicon of other languages. We have come to use these words in conversation.

**A.** Using the definitions of the boldface words, write these French words and phrases in the paragraphs.

**á la carte:** off the menu rather than part of a fixed meal
**bourgeois:** middle-class; concerned with making money
**cachet:** prestige
**cordon bleu:** "blue ribbon"; of excellent quality
**cul-de-sac:** a street closed at one end
**détente:** relaxation of tensions
**entrepreneur:** one who undertakes the risks of an enterprise
**fait accompli:** a thing accomplished and presumably irreversible
**faux pas:** a "false step"; "an error"; often said in reference to an error in manners
**gauche:** crude
**impasse:** a deadlock
**laissez-faire:** a philosophy of noninvolvement
**malaise:** unease
**nom de plume:** pen name; pseudonym
**nouveau riche** (*pl.* nouveaux riches): a class of newly wealthy people versus those from moneyed backgrounds
**par excellence:** being the best of a kind
**piece de resistance:** masterpiece
**savoir faire:** capacity for appropriate action, particularly sureness in social behavior
**tête-a-tête:** a private conversation between two people
**tour de force:** a feat of strength, skill, or ingenuity

Wilt looked with satisfaction at his new undertaking: a fine-food restaurant located in a _____ neighborhood. He hoped to attract the _____, who were moving into this once-industrial town. The building was situated in a _____, which meant there was not much drive-by traffic. Wilt was counting on the chef's reputation for presenting _____ dishes to bring in business. His _____ had been hiring Marika away from his rival's establishment. Her desserts frequently were ordered _____ by patrons too rushed to sit down for a full meal. Happily, Marika was a professional _____. She had demanded an enormous salary, but was willing to stay up all night working on her _____, a cake for the mayor's inauguration.

Although some neighbors had first objected to having a business on their street, the _____ attitude of the planning board spread to the residents, who realized that the restaurant might lend a certain _____ to the slightly run-down neighborhood. By the time the matter had come to a vote, it was a _____. Wilt had already begun renovations.

Unfortunately, the _____ made a _____ in suggesting that the large painting the neighbors had sent to welcome him was too _____ for his restaurant.

**B.** On another piece of paper, complete this story using the French words and phrases not used in Exercise A.

32  Vocabulary Practice 31: Specialized Vocabulary © Prentice-Hall, Inc.

Name _____  Date _____

# Spelling Practice 1: Prefixes and Hyphens

A prefix is usually added to a word or word part to make a new word. For some words, a hyphen is used to add the prefix to the word.

**Examples:** Use a hyphen in words that begin with a capital letter such as *mid-Victorian* and *un-American*; with the prefix *self* as in *self-made*, *self-taught*; with the prefix *ex-* meaning "former" as in *ex-champion*; in certain words with the prefix *anti-* as in *anti-hero, anti-intellectual*; to avoid confusion when a prefix ends with the same letter that the word begins with as in *co-op, de-emphasize*; when the prefix *re-* means "again" to avoid confusion with another spelling as in *re-coil* (coil again), *recoil* (draw back).

**A.** Add the prefix to the word, using a hyphen, if necessary. Write the new word. Check your answers in a dictionary.

*ex-* and *senator* _____   *anti-* and *inflammatory* _____

*re-* and *dress* _____   *ex-* and *official* _____

*ex-* and *patriate* _____   *anti-* and *coagulant* _____

*co-* and *ordination* _____   *anti-* and *establishment* _____

*re-* and *treat* _____   *de-* and *emphasize* _____

*pro-* and *European* _____   *un-* and *tenable* _____

*de-* and *escalation* _____   *pro-* and *democracy* _____

*self-* and *imposed* _____   *anti-* and *theft* _____

**B.** Write the words with the prefixes in these sentences.

1. The _____ repeated her staunch support of her former rival.
2. _____ sentiment increased after the adoption of a common currency.
3. The _____ of hostilities was a sign that the diplomats' work was worthwhile.
4. Chad's _____ isolation surprised his friends, who knew him to be an extrovert.
5. The _____ drug did not improve Mr. Winn's arthritic condition.
6. Monica's strict discipline and practice of her dance routine resulted in _____.
7. Tenants vacated the apartments because the lease was _____.
8. The _____ device did not prevent the car from being stolen.
9. A _____ movement began with small groups of students across the country.
10. The newspaper printed an article to _____ the nation's economic downturn.

**C.** Write a sentence using each word not used in Exercise B.

_____
_____
_____
_____
_____

© Prentice-Hall, Inc.

Name _____  Date _____

# Spelling Practice 2: Adding Prefixes

**Spelling Rules**

1. When a prefix is added to a word, the spelling of the word remains the same.

    **Example:** Adding the prefix *in-* to *sensitive* makes *insensitive*.

2. Some words result in double consonants when a prefix is added.

    **Example:** Adding the prefix *mis-* to *spell* makes *misspell*.

**A.** Combine the prefix and the stem and write the new word.

1. *non* and *speculative* _____
2. *un* and *scrupulous* _____
3. *im* and *potent* _____
4. *in* and *consequential* _____
5. *mis* and *apprehend* _____
6. *extra* and *curricular* _____
7. *semi* and *conscious* _____
8. *in* and *defensible* _____
9. *super* and *absorbent* _____
10. *un* and *impeachable* _____
11. *sub* and *paragraph* _____
12. *re* and *submission* _____
13. *extra* and *galactic* _____
14. *mis* and *inform* _____
15. *un* and *solicited* _____
16. *re* and *vaccinate* _____
17. *semi* and *classical* _____
18. *non* and *regulated* _____
19. *super* and *charge* _____
20. *mis* and *classify* _____
21. *non* and *venomous* _____
22. *sub* and *literate* _____
23. *anti* and *inflammatory* _____
24. *counter* and *argument* _____
25. *contra* and *indication* _____
26. *sub* and *specialist* _____
27. *fore* and *sight* _____
28. *ultra* and *conservative* _____
29. *intra* and *mural* _____
30. *counter* and *surveillance* _____
31. *macro* and *biology* _____
32. *micro* and *organism* _____
33. *inter* and *disciplinary* _____
34. *anti* and *poverty* _____
35. *pro* and *active* _____
36. *mono* and *syllable* _____
37. *inter* and *national* _____
38. *uni* and *cellular* _____
39. *post* and *traumatic* _____
40. *mega* and *byte* _____

**B.** Write these misspelled words correctly.

1. overeliance _____
2. ilogical _____
3. imobilize _____
4. imethodical _____
5. iliterate _____
6. iregular _____
7. disoluable _____
8. unatural
9. ilegible _____
10. imaterial _____
11. irevocable _____
12. imeasurable _____
13. unerving _____
14. iresolvable _____
15. ilegitimate _____

# Spelling Practice 2: Adding Prefixes

**C.** Combine the prefixes with these root words. Some prefixes can be combined with more than one word. Check your answers in a dictionary.

| sub- | im- | ag- | as- |
|---|---|---|---|
| in- | ir- | al- | at- |
| suf- | ac- | an- | macro- |
| il- | ad- | ap- | micro- |
| ig- | af- | ar- | mega- |

1. zero _____
2. arctic _____
3. literate _____
4. marine _____
5. fix _____
6. eligible _____
7. noble _____
8. firm _____
9. scribe _____
10. revocable _____
11. migrant _____
12. byte _____
13. economics _____
14. custom _____
15. vantage _____
16. join _____
17. mission _____
18. count _____
19. locate _____
20. notation _____
21. portion _____
22. range _____
23. rears _____
24. certain _____
25. tend _____
26. grieve _____
27. fuse _____
28. dose _____
29. logical _____
30. mixture _____

**D.** Circle the prefixed word that is misspelled in each sentence. Write the word correctly at the end of the sentence.

1. The impostor proclaimed his decision imutable even though it would immobilize the economy. _____

2. The illustrious author was ineligible for the award because his manuscript was ilegible. _____

3. The banker encountered an old acquaintance and recounted how the latest acquisitions affected his acounts. _____

4. The imigrants suffered disproportionately when the voting districts were illegally redrawn. _____

5. The irresolvable conflict left both parties agrieved. _____

6. The spectator was affronted when the ireverent speaker claimed that all ideas but his were illogical. _____

7. In order to addminister the program, the director subdivided the list by addresses. _____

8. The irresponsible driver was arested for flouting the irksome law. _____

9. Light suffused the room, illuminating the iresistible smile on the child's face. _____

10. The researcher studying the microrganisms aboard the submarine was inundated with questions about her discovery. _____

© Prentice-Hall, Inc.

Spelling Practice 2: Adding Prefixes  **35**

Name _____  Date _____

# Spelling Practice 3: Adding Suffixes

Adding a suffix to a base word sometimes requires a change in the spelling of the base word.

**Spelling Rules for Adding Suffixes to Words with Final *e* or Final *y***

**1.** The spelling of words that do not end in *y* does not change when adding *-ly* or *-ness*.

   **Example:** Adding *-ly* to *usual* makes *usually*.

**2.** Change *y* to *i* before adding *-ful, -ly, -ment,* or *-ness*. One-syllable words ending in *y* usually do not change to *i* before adding suffixes.

   **Example:** Adding *-ly* to *steady* makes *steadily*.
   **Example:** Adding *-ness* to *shy* makes *shyness*.

**3.** In words ending in a consonant and *y*, change *y* to *i* before adding a suffix not beginning with a consonant.

   **Examples:** Adding *-ness* to *lively* makes *liveliness*. Adding *-ness* to *wordy* makes *wordiness*.

**4.** Keep the final *e* before adding a suffix beginning with a consonant.

   **Example:** Adding *-ful* to *use* makes *useful*.
   **Exception:** Adding *-ly* to *true* makes *truly*.

**5.** Drop the final *e* before adding a suffix beginning with a vowel

   **Examples:** Adding *-ing* to *dine* makes *dining*. Adding *-able* to *debate* makes *debatable*.

(Note: There are some words that have more than one acceptable spelling: *usable* and *useable*.)

**A.** Combine the following base words and suffixes to make new words. Check your spelling in a dictionary.

1. *convalesce* and *-ence* _____
2. *precipitate* and *-ly* _____
3. *genuine* and *-ness* _____
4. *vile* and *-est* _____
5. *virtue* and *-ous* _____
6. *eerie* and *-ly* _____
7. *house* and *-ful* _____
8. *disparage* and *-ment* _____
9. *debilitate* and *-ing* _____
10. *dirge* and *-ful* _____
11. *astute* and *-ly* _____
12. *effusive* and *-ness* _____
13. *sure* and *-ty* _____
14. *pine* and *-ing* _____
15. *guile* and *-less* _____
16. *abate* and *-ment* _____
17. *effervesce* and *-ence* _____
18. *desire* and *-ous* _____
19. *revenge* and *-ful* _____
20. *antiquate* and *-ed* _____

**B.** Make two new words from each base word by adding two of the following suffixes: *-ful, -ly, -ment, -ness*.

1. *merry* and _____ makes _____
2. *stealthy* and _____ makes _____
3. *fancy* and _____ makes _____
4. *racy* and _____ makes _____
5. *wry* and _____ makes _____

# Spelling Practice 3: Adding Suffixes

**C.** For each spelling rule in Exercise A, write two words. Label the words for the spelling rule that applies.

Name _____  Date _____

# Spelling Practice 4: Adding Suffixes

**Spelling Rules**

1. Drop final *e* when adding a suffix beginning with a vowel, except when words end in *ce* or *ge*.

    **Example:** Adding *-able* to *erase* makes *erasable*.

2. Keep final *e* in words ending in *ce* or *ge* when adding a suffix beginning with *a* or *o* to retain the soft sound of *c* or *g*. Drop final *e* before suffixes beginning with *e*, *i*, or *y*.

    **Examples:** Adding *-ous* to *advantage* makes *advantageous*. Adding *-able* to *salvage* makes *salvageable*. Adding *-ed* or *-ing* to *manage* makes *managed, managing*.

3. Double the final consonent before adding a suffix beginning with a *vowel* when the last syllable is consonant-vowel-consonant and is stressed. Do not double the final consonant when the stress is on a different syllable.

    **Examples:** Adding *-er* to *begin* makes *beginner*. Adding *-able* to *regret* makes *regrettable*. Adding *-ence* or *occur* makes *occurrence*. Adding *-ed* to *rival* makes *rivaled* (unstressed final syllable).

**A.** Combine the base word with the suffix to make a new word. Check your spelling in a dictionary.

1. *embrace* and *able* _____
2. *libel* and *ous* _____
3. *trace* and *able* _____
4. *deter* and *ence* _____
5. *refer* and *al* _____
6. *manage* and *able* _____
7. *remit* and *ance* _____
8. *service* and *able* _____
9. *suffer* and *ance* _____
10. *debate* and *able* _____
11. *binge* and *ing* _____
12. *exchange* and *able* _____
13. *sulfur* and *ous* _____
14. *biodegrade* and *able* _____
15. *replace* and *able* _____
16. *assure* and *ance* _____
17. *courage* and *ous* _____
18. *abhor* and *ence* _____
19. *renew* and *able* _____
20. *disadvantage* and *ous* _____
21. *unstop* and *able* _____
22. *recur* and *ence* _____
23. *adhere* and *ence* _____
24. *dispense* and *able* _____
25. *regret* and *able* _____

**B.** Categorize the words you wrote in Exercise A according to the spelling rule that applies.

**Final *e***

_____
_____
_____
_____
_____

**Double Final Consonant**

_____
_____
_____
_____
_____

Name _____  Date _____

# Spelling Practice 5: Doubled Middle Consonants

The doubled middle consonant is essential as a marker of the preceding vowel sound. Without the doubled consonant, the pronunciation and meaning are different. The doubled middle consonant retains the short vowel sound.

**Example:** The word *caned* means "to beat with a cane," while the word *canned* means "to put in a can."

**A.** Write the word that completes the sentence.

1. Danny was _____ to get to the game on time, so when he got stuck in traffic, he was _____ mad! **hoping, hopping**

2. My favorite place to have _____ is the family-owned _____ in town. **diner, dinner**

3. Caitlin was _____ around all afternoon because her mother asked her to do some _____ of the floor. **moping, mopping**

4. When Mr. Johnson was _____ the home renovation, he included money for sanding the floors and _____ the doors. **planing, planning**

5. The entertainment reporter reported that she had a _____ of the movie star _____ in a cafe in Paris. **siting, sitting**

**B.** Circle the word that belongs with the phrase.

1. **mated/matted** fur
2. **taping/tapping** a television show
3. **caned/canned** vegetables
4. **striped/stripped** paint
5. **sparing/sparring** boxers
6. **maned/manned** shuttle
7. **scraping/scrapping** paint
8. **riper/ripper** fruit
9. **gaping/gapping** hole
10. **stared/starred** review

**C.** Write these misspelled words correctly.

1. centenial _____
2. colosal _____
3. corode _____
4. dilema _____
5. embarass _____
6. gutural _____
7. millenium _____
8. miscelaneous _____
9. parafin _____
10. paralell _____
11. oscilate _____
12. ebulient _____
13. emolient _____
14. flacid _____
15. hemorhage _____
16. curicular _____
17. exageration _____
18. harasment _____
19. paralelism _____
20. permisible _____

# Spelling Practice 5: Doubled Middle Consonants

**D.** Underline the misspelled word in each sentence and write the word correctly at the end of the sentence.

1. The visitor's scintilating conversation kept up enthralled for hours. _____
2. The telecommunications satelite was programmed to circle the earth for two years. _____
3. The environmentalists established workable guidelines to control the polution from the rubber manufacturer. _____
4. Mr. Higgins has been hired to manage the personel office for the new software development company. _____
5. On the first day of class, our English professor handed out the sylabus for the next term. _____
6. The diving team worked for months in an effort to resurect the old schooner. _____
7. In the world of baseball legends, Mickey Mantle is a perenial favorite. _____
8. When Miguel was car shopping, he vacilated between two different brands. _____
9. The landscape artist insisted on perfect symetry when arranging the plantings. _____
10. Although our vacation was uneventful, Jonah insisted upon embelishing his account of the trip. _____

**E.** List the words from Exercise D according to the doubled middle consonant letter. Then, using the dictionary, add one word with the same doubled middle consonant to each group of words.

_____
_____
_____
_____
_____
_____
_____
_____
_____
_____
_____

Name _____   Date _____

# Spelling Practice 6: Unpronounced Consonants

**Spelling Rules**
1. Unpronounced letter at the *beginning* of words.
   **Example:** *knee*
2. Unpronounced letter *b* and *n* at the end of words
   **Example:** *bomb*
3. The letters *g* and *h* are unpronounced in certain words.
   **Example:** *eighth, sign*

**A.** Write each word correctly. Then, write the rule number that applies to the spelling of the word.

1. exilarate _____
2. autum _____
3. nowledge _____
4. retched _____
5. reumatism _____
6. silouette _____
7. sychology _____
8. narled _____
9. succum _____
10. hym _____
11. hemorrage _____
12. exaustive _____
13. malin _____
14. salm _____
15. nuckle _____

**B.** Write each misspelled word correctly. Then, write two other words with the same unpronounced consonant.

1. saccarine _____
2. seudonym _____
3. nash _____
4. tyme _____
5. sychodrama _____
6. rubarb _____
7. exibitor _____
8. veement _____
9. veicle _____
10. raith _____

© Prentice-Hall, Inc.

Name _____     Date _____

# Spelling Practice 7: Spelling Word Endings

When a suffix is added to a word, the spelling of the word ending may change.

**A.** Add the suffixes to the words and write the new words. Apply spelling rules for adding suffixes.

**Example:** *adventure* and *-ous* make adventurous

1. *calamity* and *-ous* _____
2. *pity* and *-ious* _____
3. *gas* and *-eous* _____
4. *tremor* and *-ous* _____
5. *omnivore* and *-ous* _____
6. *blasphemy* and *-ous* _____
7. *outrage* and *-ous* _____
8. *fallacy* and *-ous* _____
9. *auspice* and *-ious* _____
10. *advantage* and *-ous* _____
11. *felicity* and *-ous* _____
12. *solicit* and *-ous* _____
13. *gratuity* and *-ous* _____
14. *carnivore* and *-ous* _____
15. *traitor* and *-ous* _____
16. *labor* and *-ious* _____
17. *bounty* and *-eous* _____
18. *circuit* and *-ous* _____
19. *auspice* and *-ious* _____
20. *beauty* and *-eous* _____
21. *venom* and *-ous* _____
22. *ardor* and *-ous* _____
23. *rampage* and *-ous* _____
24. *sanguine* and *-ous* _____
25. *virtue* and *-ous* _____

**B.** Add the suffix *-acious*, *-cious*, *-eous*, *-ious*, or *-ous* and write the new word. Check your spelling in a dictionary or a thesaurus.

| Word | Definition or Synonym |
| --- | --- |
| 1. lugubr _____ | sorrowful, mournful |
| 2. extemporan _____ | unrehearsed |
| 3. perfid _____ | disloyal, faithless |
| 4. capac _____ | large, roomy |
| 5. amorph _____ | having no definite form |
| 6. diaphan _____ | delicate |
| 7. egreg _____ | conspicuously bad |
| 8. fatu _____ | foolishly self-satisfied |
| 9. capri _____ | means impulsive |
| 10. gratuit _____ | unnecessary *and* unjustified |
| 11. malodor _____ | foul-smelling |
| 12. ubiquit _____ | being everywhere simultaneously |
| 13. impecun _____ | poor; having no money |
| 14. dextr _____ | skilled physically or mentally |
| 15. obsequ _____ | overly submissive |
| 16. salubr _____ | healthful |
| 17. cacophon _____ | unpleasantly noisy |
| 18. sag _____ | shrewd |
| 19. menda _____ | dishonest |
| 20. obstreper _____ | troublesome; boisterous |

42  Spelling Practice 7: Spelling Word Endings          © Prentice-Hall, Inc.

# Spelling Practice 8: Spelling Word Endings

**A.** Combine the word part and the word ending and write each word. Use the synonyms or definitions for clues. Consult a dictionary or a thesaurus, if necessary.

    *-able*        *-ible*

1. irasc _____ easily angered
2. culp _____ guilty
3. intract _____ not easily managed
4. access _____ available; attainable
5. intermin _____ endless
6. palp _____ obvious; real
7. cred _____ plausible
8. impecc _____ flawless
9. inoper _____ incurable by surgery
10. feas _____ possible
11. flamm _____ combustible
12. neglig _____ not worth considering
13. inconceiv _____ impossible
14. gull _____ easily deceived
15. amen _____ agreeable

**B.** Combine the word part and the word ending and write each word. Use the synonyms or definitions for clues. Consult a dictionary or a thesaurus, if necessary.

    *-ance*      *-ant*      *-ence*      *-ent*

1. benefic _____ kindly
2. exorbit _____ extravagant
3. eloqu _____ fluent and effective speech
4. flamboy _____ flashy; garish
5. intransig _____ uncompromising
6. forbear _____ patience; restraint
7. circumfer _____ boundary around a circle
8. belliger _____ hostile
9. discord _____ harsh-sounding
10. endur _____ ability to withstand hardships
11. somnol _____ sleepy; drowsy
12. convales _____ gradual recovery from illness
13. effervesc _____ bubbly; lively
14. incess _____ continuous
15. luxuri _____ elegance; lavishness

Name _____  Date _____

# Spelling Practice: Spelling Review

**A.** Rewrite the misspelled words correctly. Check the words in a dictionary. Put a check (√) next to the words spelled correctly.

1. exumed _____
2. concieve _____
3. insidious _____
4. acnowledgement _____
5. wrily _____
6. rheumatism _____
7. silouette _____
8. aqueous _____
9. nausious _____
10. umbragious _____
11. acquaintence _____
12. cemetary _____
13. secretary _____
14. advantageous _____
15. ambitous _____
16. vengance _____
17. indefensible _____
18. amenible _____
19. debateable _____
20. incontrovertable _____
21. ilimitable _____
22. erronious _____
23. marriageable _____
24. imortalize _____
25. flacid _____
26. desireous _____
27. immethodical _____
28. virulent _____
29. somnolant _____
30. hideous _____

**B.** Circle the misspelled words. Write them correctly at the end of the sentences.

1. Treating the hemorrage exausted the resources of the understaffed hospital. _____

2. Solving the thorny dilema exilerated the normally complacent research scientist. _____

3. Calling the project a collosal failure was an exageration, although the negligable positive effects of the formula were disappointing. _____

4. In autumm, the farmer cut down the narled apple trees. _____

5. The personell director vascilated between the two candidates for the executive position. _____

6. The cost of the proceedure exceded the limits imposed by the mangement commitee. _____

7. The attorney interceeded on behalf of the unmanagable client who was prone to vehement outbursts. _____

8. The salacious gossip of the radio host malined the reputation of the area's pre-eminant psychologist. _____

9. The director recreated the titilating scene from the highly aclaimed foregn novel. _____

10. The boxing referree intervened before the champion's opponent succumed to his debilitating injuries. _____

44  Spelling Practice: Spelling Review                                    © Prentice-Hall, Inc.